THE COMING WORLD

BY CHRISTOPHER SHINN

★

DRAMATISTS
PLAY SERVICE
INC.

THE COMING WORLD
Copyright © 2001, 2003, Christopher Shinn

All Rights Reserved

SPECIAL NOTE

First performed by Soho Theatre Company.

Sure, what do you care for money? You'd give your last penny to the first beggar you met, if he had a shotgun pointed at your heart.

—*Eugene O'Neill*
A Moon for the Misbegotten

… This music's almost unrecognizable, so utterly of the coming world it is.

—*Mark Doty*
"Tunnel Music"

A NOTE ON THE DESIGN

I am not a designer but it is, I think, worth noting that as I wrote this play, I imagined it taking place on a bare stage (no sand!), with no costume change or use of makeup effects, etc. While the play may benefit from a careful nod towards more traditional design elements, it's important that they not overwhelm the text which, I think, can tell us more than showing can.

In the London production there were no sound effects or music; no makeup effects; basic lighting, bright (though the play takes place largely at night); and a mostly bare stage made of grey wooden planks. Scenes in the ocean were created by taking out all lights; the actors held thin flashlights which washed light over their bodies. What I would stress most is that the play mustn't get lost in darkness and night. The text tells the audience it's evening; the lights should let us see clearly those evenings play out.

A NOTE ON THE TEXT

Dialogue in the play often overlaps, and a slash (/) indicates where the character who speaks next begins. In the second scene, I use punctuation to convey a sense of the unspoken. The meaning should be clear to both the actors and the audience, while maintaining the idiosyncratic and intimate system of communication the lovers use in their distress. Sometimes it's used to portray a gap in communication, a pregnant nonspoken moment different from a flat pause. Other times, a manner of speech is conveyed. For instance, if the dialogue in the text reads

DORA. (You said) What?

The actress would speak, and the audience would hear:

DORA. What?

The parentheses are meant to clarify the meaning of what is actually spoken (rather than implied), to avoid a situation where an actor would say:

DORA. What?

And the audience would understand it to mean:

DORA. What (do you mean)?

THE COMING WORLD was originally produced by the Soho Theatre Company in London, England, opening on April 3, 2001. It was directed by Mark Brickman; the set design was by Michael Pavelka; the lighting design was by Jason Taylor; and the stage manager was Lorraine Tozer. The cast was as follows:

ED/TY .... Andrew Scott
DORA .... Doraly Rosen

CHARACTERS

ED

DORA

TY

Ed and Ty are played by the same actor.

PLACE

Summer, on a beach on the coast of New England.

TIME

Summer 2001.

THE COMING WORLD

SCENE ONE

The beach. Dora and Ed are laughing.

ED. Come on, dare me.
DORA. "Dare" you!
ED. Fifty more! *(Flicking a little handful of sand at her.)* Come/on!
DORA. *(Laughing.)* Ah! Don't throw sand at me! — Go ahead, torture yourself.
ED. Here we go. *One ... (Ed does push-ups. Dora brushes sand out of her hair.)*
DORA. Hey, the DVDs are coming in a couple weeks, they called today.
ED. No shit!
DORA. They're starting slow, building them in slow. They did a survey I guess, and not that many people here have DVD players yet.
ED. Yeah, 'cuz there's no fucking place to buy DVDs! What am I at, forty?
DORA. Yeah, *right.* That's gonna be a pain, though, building them in, we're gonna have to totally rearrange the store to make room for new shelves. *(He stops and catches his breath.)*
ED. What are we doing tonight?
DORA. I dunno. Why don't we just stay on the beach, it's nice.
ED. You're not working tomorrow, right?
DORA. At night I am. I'm closing.
ED. Get some drinks?
DORA. We could watch a movie ...

ED. Go out, have a couple gin and tonics …
DORA. When is it ever "a couple." All night.
ED. I'm not saying all night. Plus — Martin's gonna be out tonight.
DORA. Martin? *(Ed starts doing push-ups again.)*
ED. You remember Martin.
DORA. Yeah, no shit. Why, what about him?
ED. They're hiring. He said — at the — they need money/runners
DORA. You're not gonna fucking work at the casino.
ED. Maybe — not, like, right away. But — enough time's passed, right?
DORA. Every day going there?
ED. The pay is so good. They're hiring. Where/else
DORA. So, if you gamble it, so, who cares how much the pay is, you know?
ED. Gambling wasn't — it was the coke that was the thing. The gambling wasn't — I don't even like gambling. Plus I feel *so* much better now —
DORA. That's what I'm saying, you're feeling so much better, so why put yourself back there? *(Pause.)*
ED. It's just drinks, I mean — I don't even know — it's not like I got the job.
DORA. No, I don't wanna go out drinking tonight. *(Pause.)*
ED. All right. The thing is …
DORA. You told Martin already. *(Pause.)* So cancel.
ED. Dora —
DORA. No, I worked all day, I don't/wanna
ED. I can't just/blow him off
DORA. So go without me.
ED. No … *(Pause.)*
DORA. Why not?
ED. 'Cuz I wanna be with you tonight. *(Pause.)*
DORA. All right …
ED. Uh-oh. Dora's got an idea.
DORA. I'll go out for drinks if you call Ty and invite him out. *(Pause.)*
ED. Why?
DORA. I wanna meet him! Eight months, your twin brother and

10

I have no idea what he's/like
ED. He's not gonna come out.
DORA. Why not?
ED. He doesn't *go* out.
DORA. Tell him I want to meet him. — I wanna meet the guy!
(Pause. Ed looks at the ocean. Then turns to Dora and smiles. Grabs Dora's foot and kisses it, bites it a little. She moans quietly. He licks her foot. She begins to laugh.)
ED. What's so funny? *(He tickles her foot, she shrieks, laughs.)*
DORA. No!
ED. No? No? *(He embraces her.)*
DORA. Stop! You're all smelly!
ED. I'm smelly?
DORA. Yes!
ED. Then I guess I'm gonna make *you* all smelly!
DORA. No! *(He tickles her, she shrieks with laughter. Then he stops. Then he tickles her again, she shrieks with laughter. Then he stops. He starts to tickle her again, she laughs less, as though exhausted. He stares at her a beat, then looks out at the ocean. She follows his gaze to the ocean.)*
ED. Beautiful.
DORA. It is ... *(Ed turns to her.)*
ED. No. You. You have the most beautiful face. *(Pause. Dora smiles, then turns away.)* Okay. *(Ed playfully smacks Dora's thigh.)* Call my weirdo brother for you.

SCENE TWO

The beach. Dora approaches Ed. She startles him; he jerks.

DORA. Ahh!
ED. Shit!
DORA. Ed!
ED. Sorry.

DORA. Jesus.

ED. Sorry. *(Ed looks at Dora, smiles.)*

DORA. (   ). *(Pause.)*

ED. (   )?

DORA. I don't wanna be here.

ED. I know —

DORA. I can't get in your shit now —

ED. Nothing for you to get into ... Sit.

DORA. I'm just — if you want something (just tell me now) ...

ED. All I want — serious — all I want is to just ... (   ) ... *(She doesn't sit.)* Miss you. — Okay that I say that?

DORA. (You) Just did.

ED. Yeah.

DORA. You look bad.

ED. I look *bad?*

DORA. Yeah.

ED. It's dark!

DORA. What.

ED. I look bad (in the dark)?

DORA. *(Sitting.)* Circles under your eyes, unshaven ...

ED. Really?

DORA. Are you ... (on drugs)?

ED. No.

DORA. No?

ED. *You* look good.

DORA. I worked all day, I look tired.

ED. How was work?

DORA. (You wanna talk about) Work?

ED. What movies came in today?

DORA. They come in Tuesdays.

ED. You put them up Tuesdays, but you get them before.

DORA. (   ). *(Pause.)*

ED. (I'll) Rub your feet.

DORA. (No.)

ED. Shoulders. You look tense.

DORA. I don't (want a massage).

ED. Stressed out, standing all day, the kids, annoying, come on.

DORA. Not everyone hates their job.

ED. Thanks.

DORA. "The kids, annoying" — (actually) I like my job.

ED. Good for you. (   )?

DORA. ⊥ I'm just saying, you're making it like I hate my job.

ED. I just said do you want a massage that place stresses you out. *(Pause.)*

DORA. You have to stop calling me. *(Pause.)*

ED. Who's talking about this.

DORA. We broke up.

ED. Okay.

DORA. Okay?

ED. I just wanted to talk. Am I doing anything?

DORA. "Can I rub your feet."

ED. ?

DORA. You don't do the same things after you break up. You don't (give massages) —

ED. — I don't even feel bad.

DORA. (   )?

ED. Not about you. Something else. I mean I do (feel bad) about you. But I don't know if I (feel bad) about this other thing. Maybe after I say it I'll feel bad. — No one knows (what I did).

DORA. What are you talking/about

ED. Why do you think Ty won't talk to me?

DORA. (   ).

ED. He won't call me back. Since we hung out. Which. That was a fun night. He had fun, right?

DORA. (Like) You remember (that night).

ED. It was only a month ago.

DORA. No. Because you blacked out. (I was) Dragging you home.

ED. (You didn't) Drag me home.

DORA. Yeah (right)!

ED. He's probably just heavy into work. Computer shit. Big money. I thought it was maybe the money (he lent me) but that doesn't make sense. Why he would be mad about that.

DORA. (   )?

ED. He lent me money. I think he sent it, I think he sent it the next day, day after we hung out. We were broke up when I got the check so I didn't tell you but. In the mail. Five thousand dollars.

13

(I was like) Shit! Five thousand dollars! Just in my mail! No note, no anything, and so — I called him, to like — I don't know, to thank him or to say (why did you send me five thousand dollars) … (I keep) Calling, but he won't call me back. — Why did I get so drunk that night?

DORA. He just — (sent you) five thousand dollars. *(Pause.)* (I hope) You don't need more.

ED. *(Laughs.)* Why do you say that?

DORA. Because — you don't look so good, you don't look a guy who has five thousand dollars, so — (do you need more?) … *(Ed reaches into his pocket, takes out ten singles.)* What (are you doing).

ED. Ten dollars.

DORA. (I know) But (why)?

ED. (This is) All I have left. *(Pause.)*

DORA. (   )?

ED. It went.

DORA. I don't (understand).

ED. Paid bills, paid — not like five's a fortune, I mean, what I owe. I was just trying to set things up, climb outta this hole —

DORA. The thousand (I gave you, is that gone too)?

ED. I paid off the credit card (with that).

DORA. Where did it (go)?

ED. …

DORA. I'm not (giving you anything) — Nothing.

ED. I had a job.

DORA. ?

ED. (I got paid a) Thousand a week.

DORA. …

ED. You want me to jump to the end of the story or start at the start of it?

DORA. I don't (care).

ED. It's just, I don't know which way (makes more sense) — starting and going forward or going to the end and then back. Makes sense — (not the story, but) telling you.

DORA. I'm not going to get all (wrapped up in it) …

ED. But do you want to hear just the outcome or how I got there …

DORA. It's not gonna make me *do* something (I'm not gonna do).

ED. (Do you know) I'm the only person Ty ever showed his tattoos to? I ever tell you that?

DORA. This (relates how)? ...

ED. I'm just — trying to talk like — like there's none of this shit in between us.

DORA. (So you lost) Five thousand dollars.

ED. You think I should get a tattoo?

DORA. — They're gross.

ED. Why?

DORA. It's like self-mutilation, they're ugly.

ED. Ty showed me his. I'm the only one.

DORA. Ed. Come on. *(Ed looks at her. Pause.)*

ED. Okay. All right. (I'll tell you) What happened. *(Pause.)*

DORA. I don't need all kinds of details.

ED. All right. *(Pause. She turns.)* I just — there's this one question to get — out of the way — so I can tell you what happened because, just — I ... *(Pause.)*

DORA. ?

ED. ...

DORA. ...?

ED. No, I know (why you broke up with me). I had no money. What you (said), I have no (money), I'm in debt, I have no job, you can't be with someone (with) no money (and) no job ... But — if there's (another reason) — you can tell me, I just (wanna know) —

DORA. No, there's no other reason, Ed.

ED. All right, okay, that's all I wanted (to know) ... *(She looks out at the ocean.)* Okay. Okay. So. There's this (guy). I'm in the (casino) — at the least, I promise you, this is a good story.

DORA. *(Turning back to him.)* Then (start telling it).

ED. No, because you look like (you don't care) —

DORA. I'm (listening, just tell me).

ED. I'm just (saying) — ... Okay. — I haven't even told this (to anyone). Okay. I'm in the casino chilling, and this guy says there's this guy he knows. And the guy, the guy I'm talking to —

DORA. ?

ED. (Okay,) Martin.

DORA. Martin (great).

15

ED. Don't get all stupid.

DORA. Fucking Martin.

ED. Martin and John.

DORA. (I don't know) John (who is he)?

ED. They just know each other. John's at the casino all the time, Martin knows him from there. Okay. So Martin tells me John, John needs somebody for something — under-the — quick-buck thing. Puts me in (touch) — Martin — with John — in touch so — okay? Okay. So: what do I have to lose? I figure (what the hell, who knows) — so — okay. I call John. Hello, hello, come over, so. I go over. House, *his* house, oh my God. It's (fucking amazing) — totally new, mile away (from the casino) — inside — big TV, flat-screen, DVD. Guys watching *The Matrix* — the scene (where Neo fights the guy in the subway) — John sits me down, this *other* guy, guy gets *me* a drink, and I'm — (sitting) on this like electronic plush chair — massage, adjust the —

DORA. (What are all) These details …

ED. (Sorry, I'm getting all excited.) Okay. So. Okay. So John's like, a big guy, maybe thirty, well-groomed, but, like, hairy back kind of guy. (He's) Mob (and he's like —)

DORA. ?

ED. But (not scary).

DORA. Mob.

ED. (All right, but) He says, "It's a very simple thing, Ed." Simple. I'm like — (it's) like a movie, (I'm) sitting there, like — "I supply" — this is him — "I"

DORA. You don't have to get all dramatic.

ED. (You don't think it's funny?) — Okay. "I supply a local man with ecstasy. He distributes it to his people at six schools. I don't like to be involved with drugs but it's a lot of money and this is as far as I go with it. It's safe, it's easy, it's very lucrative. What your job is is this:" — and I'm sitting there, with my drink, thinking like (is this really happening?) — "Your job is this:" — not would be, (but) *is* — "once a week, you'll deliver the ecstasy to this man. You'll be paid a thousand for each delivery. All you do is come here, pick up a backpack with ten thousand dollars of pills, drive half an hour, hand it over, take the cash, bring it back, I'll cut you a thousand, and you'll go home." (*Pause.*) I mean, problem solved!

Before Christmas! Four thousand a month!

DORA. So you just (say yes) …

ED. (I know but) I think — what if he knows some other guy, more eager guy, I don't want to (lose the chance) — Martin (must know other guys but) — he thought of me first. John's like, "Martin speaks very highly of you."

DORA. Martin speaks highly of you. Which, he knows you from (what). "He's a good drinker. He sniffs coke and loses money really well."

ED. (Fuck you.)

DORA. (   ).

ED. (   ).

DORA. Five minutes (you know this guy) and you say yes.

ED. I thought — he needs his money — drugs need to get where they're going — (it's) simple how I fit in. John said he doesn't like his guys to do it because if you get caught it's mandatory minimum sentence, so he contracts it out to keep it out of his thing. He said no one ever got caught but it's better for him that he's not directly connected to it.

DORA. Fine, so. What (happened). (*Ed pauses, staring at Dora.*) (   )?

ED. Okay. So. Next day. I get the backpack. They give me a phone number. (Of) The guy I'm handing over to. I'm supposed to go to the payphone in the parking lot of the bank near the Burger King. I call and let it ring. I can only use that payphone because what the guy is going to do is, is look at his Caller ID, and when he sees that payphone number, he's gonna come meet me at the bank. That way there's no talking on any phones. So. I get the backpack. I get in my car and go. Get to the Burger King, the bank, pull in, pull around back …

DORA. (Wait,) What time is it?

ED. What?

DORA. Is it dark? (*Short pause.*) This is the phone, the one behind the bank, out of sight of the road?

ED. There's — the Burger King —

DORA. There's the fence between the bank and the Burger King. And it's dark. (Do you see?)

ED. What are you (saying)?

17

DORA. (You're sitting where) No one can see you.

ED. Why would you want anyone to see?

DORA. (It's a) Backpack — you could hand it over *in* the Burger/King!

ED. You wanna tell the story? You know what happens?

DORA. (   ). (*Pause.*)

ED (So I) Pick up the phone. Dial. Ringing. Then (I hear) a tap on the glass. (Out of) Nowhere. (I) Look. (It's a) Gun. Passenger side, guy with a gun, tapping on the glass. (I) Turn around, (my) window's rolled down, (I) still have the phone to my ear, sitting in the car, so my window is down, (I) turn. Another guy. (Guy) *Rips* the phone from my hand, hangs it up, slams it … (I) Give him the (backpack) … They just (go) … (*Pause. Dora looks away.*) So.

DORA. Do you know what happened?

ED. (*Grabbing stomach.*) Fuck, my stomach. Can you hear that?

DORA. What?

ED. I guess only I can hear it, 'cuz of the vibrations in my body.

DORA. What are you talking about?

ED. My stomach is making weird noises, it hurts.

DORA. — Ed, they didn't see the Caller ID, so how did they know what time you were gonna be there?

ED. I guess — I figure John probably told them around when to expect me. So they were probably just hanging out, waiting. Waiting for a car to pull in there, pick up the phone. Boom.

DORA. But … you don't see?

ED. (   )?

DORA. Okay. So — Martin and John know each other a little, they bullshit, whatever. One night John says to Martin, "Hey Martin, I need a favor." Martin's flattered, (he's a) bartender, (and a) mob guy needs his help. (He) Says, "Want you to find me some kid, some fuckup who needs some money. I'll jerk him around, scare him a little, but I won't hurt him, you have my word. You know anybody?" (You.) Now, John's got this all planned out already with the guy — the distributor guy, the dealer. John fills him in, the dealer gives him nine thousand bucks. The *dealer* gets to save a thousand, and now John has an errand boy who thinks he owes him ten thousand bucks. Who'll do whatever he wants.

ED. What…?

DORA. (They) Pumped you up, gave you a bullshit story — the whole thing was planned out. Robbing *you* works out for *both* of them, they *both* save all this money, meanwhile, *you* get a gun in your face, and now *you* think you owe a mobster ten thousand bucks. Which, if he says you do, you do. So now he'll make you work it off, doing all his dirty work or whatever.

ED. I don't … you think he set me up? But — no. No way. John — no, there's gotta be holes in there.

DORA. There's no holes.

ED. (   ). *(Short pause.)* Oh — oh fuck —

DORA. They're not stupid, these guys, they know what they're doing. This dealer is gonna rob a mobster? No one robs mobsters. They have a whole system, this whole thing together, and this guy's just gonna up and rob him? It's where he gets the ecstasy from — like you said, they both need each other.

ED. Oh God. *(Pause.)*

DORA. (Tell me the truth,) Are you doing coke?

ED. Not — really, I don't know, a couple of times —

DORA. Five thousand dollars partying.

ED. I haven't (been partying that much), I've been paying (off my debts.) — *you* doing coke?

DORA. (We're) Talking about me now?

ED. Don't be so angry.

DORA. Fine, (let's) talk about me, what do *you* want *me* to do? *(Pause.)*

ED. (   ).

DORA. So I can just leave now.

ED. All right. This is what I came up with. I thought — I can move home, (that) kills my rent, (that) kills my bills. I gotta pay John, God knows what he's gonna make me do to pay it off. So, get the ten thousand out of the way, hold off my other debts —

DORA. So, what, this ten thousand is just gonna wash up on shore?

ED. Well — I gotta find a job. Obviously.

DORA. How do I fit into this.

ED. Well … I know I can't — stay with you.

DORA. You already figured that out, you're gonna stay with your folks.

ED. Right. *(Pause.)* I know … you don't have any money I could

... (   ) ...

DORA. (   ).

ED. I know.

DORA. So all that's left that I can do for you is fuck you, basically.

ED. (Seriously)?

DORA. !

ED. Kidding Dora! I'm not (that dumb). But what's going on with you, you seeing anybody?

DORA. (   ).

ED. I hope he's good to you, that's all I hope.

DORA. (I) Got it.

ED. What?

DORA. Ask Ty for more money.

ED. No.

DORA. Why not?

ED. That's not right.

DORA. Why not?

ED. No!

DORA. He gave you five thousand.

ED. I didn't ask for it. He just gave it to me.

DORA. So?

ED. What I don't understand is. Because you said you loved me. So when. How do you just stop. Two people/who

DORA. (   ).

ED. If you loved me one month/ago

DORA. Ed

ED. Do you love me? (*Pause.*) *Did* you?

DORA. (   ).

ED. ?

DORA. Yes (but) —

ED. So when did you stop.

DORA. (   ). (*Pause.*)

ED. I'm sorry.

DORA. I'm gonna/leave, Ed.

ED. Okay, wait. Wait. I got this idea. It's a way you can help me. It's a really good idea. (*Dora looks at Ed. Ed looks at Dora.*) I wanna. Okay. Ready?

DORA. (   ).

ED. I wanna rob the Blockbuster.

DORA. — What?

ED. How much is it before you put the final night's total in the safe?

DORA. Ed.

ED. Corporation, won't feel a thing. A couple thousand, right? At closing, so easy, just you in the store —

DORA. No, Ed!

ED. I know there's all those cameras and stuff, but I put on a mask or whatever, we make it look like an actual robbery, like, with a gun and stuff, simple!

DORA. A *gun?*

ED. I have one. I got one.

DORA. You have a *gun?*

ED. What if I get into trouble with John? (What if I have to do) Some ghetto shit? *(Pause.)*

DORA. I'm going, Ed.

ED. You're gonna go. You're just gonna go.

DORA. *(Rising.)* Yeah.

ED. All right. Whatever. *(Starts removing clothes.)* Thanks for the help!

DORA. What are you doing?

ED. (I'm gonna) Take a swim. You wanna?

DORA. Fuck you. *(Dora starts to exit. Ed stands naked, laughs.)*

ED. You know you want me. That's why you're leaving! *(She keeps going till she is off. Calling:)* You know that's why you're leaving! Come on, come swimming with me. *(Pause. Dora is off. He yells:)* WHY DON'T YOU COME BACK HERE AND COME SWIMMING WITH ME. WHY DON'T YOU COME BACK AND SUCK MY DICK LIKE YOU USED TO! *(Long pause. He's still watching. Screaming:)* WHY DON'T YOU COME BACK AND TELL ME YOU LOVE ME. *(Hold.)*

SCENE THREE

Ty approaches Dora on the beach, tentatively.

TY. Dora? *(She turns, startled.)*
DORA. Oh — I didn't … *(She stands with some difficulty.)* Hey Ty.
TY. Hi. — Are you okay?
DORA. I'm okay.
TY. Jesus.
DORA. It's not that bad. They got me on Vicodin, so …
TY. What happened?
DORA. You don't know? You didn't hear?
TY. No.
DORA. The Blockbuster got robbed. *(Pause.)*
TY. Oh.
DORA. Didn't get any money actually. But I got roughed up …
TY. Oh my God.
DORA. I thought everybody heard.
TY. No, I …
DORA. Don't talk to anybody?
TY. *(Smiles.)* Right. *(Dora sits, with some difficulty.)*
DORA. I figured your parents would have told you. Just some random thing — it happens — just happened to happen to me, so.
TY. Does it hurt?
DORA. Just normal pain.
TY. What's normal pain?
DORA. Just — you know. Pain you can live with. *(Short pause.)* I just — wanted to talk to someone.
TY. Sure.
DORA. Because — I didn't — feel like I could go to the wake. I was gonna, but. Your folks didn't — they always said to Eddie how I was "loud." And Eddie's friends … Eddie partied so much less when he was with me so they … I would have just gone in, fuck 'em, but — my face …

TY. Right.

DORA. They don't — the Doctors don't know what it's gonna look like yet ... *(Short pause.)* Anyway, I just kept — all night, driving by the funeral home. His buddies outside smoking. Called information, got your number, left you that message, and just came here and ... — What — was it — nice, or? ... The wake, what was it like?

TY. Actually ... I didn't go.

DORA. You didn't go?

TY. Same thing basically. Ed's friends, I can't stand those guys. And I guess Ed never told you, but I don't — I don't speak to my folks.

DORA. Oh. I didn't know that. Why not?

TY. We just don't get along.

DORA. Uh-huh. *(Pause.)* I actually — I called you because — when I was driving by, like, the funeral home, I kept, I kept thinking about something you said. That night we all went out.

TY. What?

DORA. That's the thing. It's like, I can't remember it! You talk so good — I can't talk that good. But it was something like — remember, Eddie was getting drinks, or in the bathroom or something and you said — it was so loud and dark — in the bar — and I was like, Why, if you want to hang out with your friends, why would you come to a place like this? Where it's so loud you can't hear them and so dark you can't see them. — Do you remember what you said?

TY. I think ... I said that guys don't like to talk.

DORA. Yeah. But you kept going.

TY. Well, that they go out because they're looking for a girl to sleep with or a guy to fight.

DORA. Yeah, no, it was after that.

TY. Right — that they communicate with actions. Not words. Guys.

DORA. Yeah! That was it. That's so right, like. And it came back to me — because I was thinking — what you said, with Eddie. Like — what was it Eddie couldn't say. That he would do this. *(Short pause.)* That he'd — shoot himself. *(Short pause.)*

TY. I don't know. Ed was never the most — rational guy ...

DORA. No ...

TY. Just — spending that one night with him. He was a mess.

DORA. Yeah. I actually broke up with him the next day.

TY. You did?

DORA. You didn't know that?

TY. No, I — no.

DORA. I didn't know if you talked to him in the time … between … then/and —

TY. Right.

DORA. Did you?

TY. What?

DORA. Talk to him at all or…?

TY. I — a few nights ago — he showed up at my apartment sort of — out of the blue …

DORA. What was …

TY. Just. Um. Well. Really, he seemed just — basically like he was fucked up on a lot of drugs. He didn't make much — sense …

DORA. That was it?

TY. Yeah …

DORA. That fucking night. After you left. It was horrible. Eddie kept drinking, right. Then this guy Martin showed up, like three hours later than he was supposed to. Do you know this guy?

TY. No.

DORA. Martin. Works at the casino, he's a bartender, and Eddie — thought he might help him get a job there, right? So we're talking and drinking and Eddie keeps, like, bringing up jobs and stuff, but Martin's not — he's not saying anything about jobs, right? Then Martin kinda leans in and says, "Wanna know a secret?" And Eddie's like, "Sure." And Martin says, "You know why you get so many free drinks in a casino?" And Eddie's like, "Because the drunker you are, the more you'll gamble." And Martin gets all quiet, like he's being all bad by telling us this, and says, "No." He says, "We want, we give out free drinks because we want you to feel like everyone here is your friend." *(Pause.)* "We do it so you'll associate the casino with getting something for free, with generosity. That's what makes you gamble more. We actually don't want you drunk, we actually pump oxygen into the casino to keep you sober and awake." And Martin *laughs.* I think it's gross, this guy, talking about how they trick people into losing their money, but I look at Eddie — and Eddie's got this look on his face like — he's entranced. Like this is the coolest thing. But Eddie — I'm thinking, like — Eddie works hard. All his jobs, you can't fuck anyone over in those jobs, they can just fuck you. Eddie moves boxes. Eddie drives trucks, mows lawns, plows snow. Eddie gets fucked over all the time, so — why does he think this is all cool? Anyway, the night goes on — Martin doesn't say a *word* about any job. Takes out a bag of coke, Eddie's eyes go real big, like — that was it. Dragged him out of there, drove him home, puking in my car, put him in bed, and left. *(Pause.)* And … that was the last time I saw him. That night. Blacked out, puking all over himself. Called him the next day and dumped him.

TY. I actually — sent him some money after that night.

DORA. You did?

TY. Just to — I don't know what. Something … *(Pause.)*

DORA. I told Eddie to invite you out that night. I wanted to meet you. He was kinda weird about it. He didn't talk about you a lot.

TY. Didn't have much in common.

DORA. Eddie said you're like a genius.

TY. He said that? That's funny. He never really understood what I do. It's pretty simple.

DORA. You work really hard though, right?

TY. Not really.

DORA. Yeah right.

TY. No, I just have a skill most people don't.

DORA. What exactly do you do?

TY. You really want to know?

DORA. Yeah.

TY. It's pretty boring.

DORA. No, what *I* do is boring.

TY. *(Laughs.)* I design educational programming for use in schools.

DORA. Uh-huh?

TY. Which means — I take what would have been a schoolbook, and put it on a computer screen. So what I'm really doing is taking what something is — the content — and changing the look of it — the form — to fit a different medium.

DORA. Uh-huh …

TY. I'm making it sound more complicated than it is. Like — all right: you have computers at Blockbuster, right? What do they do?

25

DORA. The computers. Just — keep track of your account. What you rented, if it's overdue, like that.

TY. Exactly. Those are primitive programs — meaning they do simple tasks — but even so — think about before those computers. Someone would have had to write down all the information, what you rented, when it was due, and store it in a file cabinet, and retrieving that information would have taken time and slowed down the business … so, now, instead of lots of file cabinets and paper cuts and hand cramps, you have a computer on a desk and sore wrists and tired eyes. What I do is, instead of a kid sitting in a classroom, with ink all over his hands and seven books in his backpack, and five notebooks for his different classes — instead, he's tapping away at a computer. I'm sort of the bridge between the past and the future — or the file cabinet and the computer.

DORA. I have no idea what you just said.

TY. *(Laughs.)* Meaning, we're not there yet. Kids still have books. They still write notes in notebooks with pens. But they won't always. Someday, they'll type notes onto a computer, and read lessons on a screen, and the teacher will type lessons during class, which they'll read on their screen, and be able to read when they go home, because they'll be doing their homework and going over their notes on their computers at home. I'm designing the programming that will make that happen.

DORA. Wow. What's the company's name that you work for?

TY. Education Alternatives. "Preparing Children for the Coming World."

DORA. The backpack companies won't be happy. *(Laughs.)* I like my job. It's okay. People'll always wanna watch movies I guess. *(Dora clutches her jaw.)*

TY. Are you okay?

DORA. The D-d-doctor said not to. T-t-talk too much. Nnnh. *(Pause. Dora holds her jaw, in evident pain. Reaches into her purse, takes out a Vicodin pill, dry swallows it.)* I'm okay. Sometimes it throbs.

TY. What?

DORA. The pain. It just, out of nowhere, this throbbing. I'm okay. I'm fine. — You had a horrible night, too, right.

TY. What?

DORA. At the bar that night.

TY. No!

DORA. Come on, you hated it.

TY. No — it was really cool talking to you. I left because — I just couldn't watch him like that.

DORA. You were so uncomfortable like.

TY. In the bar. Yeah — it's that thing — like Eddie's friends. I just don't fit in.

DORA. Eddie loved taking me out to bars. I hated it, but. He said he always wanted to show me off. I thought that was stupid, but. I don't know, is that how guys are?

TY. Is that — are guys? …

DORA. Like, do you like showing off your girlfriends, or? …

TY. Um … I don't — I never really thought about it …

DORA. Like, do you like to go to the movies with your girl, or do you like to hang at home?

TY. I guess it — depends …

DORA. Yeah. Do you have a girlfriend now or…?

TY. No, no, not at the — … /no.

DORA. Oh — secret's out — Ty's a player!

TY. Ha!/Right!

DORA. You are, for real. I see that little grin, that's a player grin. *(Ty laughs. Then clutches his stomach.)* Are you okay?

TY. Oh, I'm fine, just — my stomach.

DORA. Is it? …

TY. It's a — I'm fine.

DORA. That's funny. Eddie had stomach things all the time.

TY. He did?

DORA. I always thought it was how much crap he ate. Do you eat, like, Burger King every day?

TY. I'm a vegetarian.

DORA. That must suck.

TY. No — it's really easy being a vegetarian. I cook/my own

DORA. No, I meant, it must suck having people always assume because you have a twin, you're the same in all these ways.

TY. Oh. Yeah. When I was a kid — I hated it. Everyone thought I liked what Eddie liked — because what Eddie liked was what everyone liked.

DORA. Is that why you got tattoos? *(Pause.)* To be different?

27

TY. How do you —?

DORA. Eddie told me. I hope it's okay that I — he was so proud, like — that you showed him your tattoos.

TY. That's — he said that?

DORA. Could I see? *(Pause.)* They're — you can't see them on your/arms

TY. I wanted them to be private.

DORA. Right.

TY. But. If you — …

DORA. It's just — I'm so curious. *(Short pause. Ty stands. Dora follows. A beat. Then Ty lifts his shirt over his head, covering his face.)* Oh my God. So many. *(Short pause. She takes his T-shirt and lifts it the rest of the way off his head, and gently lets his T-shirt fall to the ground. Ty smiles. She looks at his body.)* They're beautiful.

TY. Thanks.

DORA. What do they mean?

TY. They're j-just — abstract designs …

DORA. You're shivering.

TY. A little/cold

DORA. Did that hurt?

TY. What?

DORA. The nipple ring?

TY. Just — *(Laughs.)* just normal pain.

DORA. All down just the one side …

TY. I wanted it to be ordered — not random, all/over

DORA. He didn't tell me they were all down just the one side.

TY. That's because — actually — he never saw them actually. *(Short pause. Dora looks at him.)* He knew that I had them, but I never showed them to him. *(Short pause. She places her hand on his chest, slowly moves it down across his abdomen.)*

DORA. Where did you get them?

TY. I — I did them myself.

DORA. Wait — *you* did them?

TY. Yeah, I — bought the tools and studied and … *(Pause. They look as if about to embrace; then, Ty turns away. Dora looks out at the ocean. Ty reaches down to pick up his shirt.)*

DORA. Wanna go swimming?

TY. — Now?

DORA. You think I'm crazy?

TY. It's — a little/cold

DORA. You ever done it?

TY. Swim — in the/ocean at

DORA. At night?

TY. No.

DORA. Eddie and I used to. *(Short pause. She looks at him and smiles. Then she removes her clothes, to her undergarments.)* Coming?

TY. I ... *(Dora smiles at Ty, then runs into the ocean, off. Ty watches her for a moment. Then he takes off his pants and rushes into the ocean, off. In the ocean, we see Dora; Ty appears far behind her, slowly and blindly finding his way to her.)* OH!

DORA. TY?

TY. IT'S COLD!

DORA. TY?

TY. IT'S FREEZING!

DORA. CAN YOU SEE ME?

TY. NO!

DORA. WHERE ARE YOU?

TY. BACK HERE!

DORA. COME TO WHERE I AM! I'LL KEEP TALKING! FOLLOW THE SOUND!

TY. OKAY!

DORA. HELLO HELLO HELLO! GOODBYE GOODBYE GOODBYE!

TY. ... GETTING CLOSER.

DORA. I HEAR YOU BETTER. HELLO HELLO HELLO!

TY. HELLO HELLO HELLO!

DORA. SEAWEED! SEAWEED! SEASHELL! SEASHELL!

TY. Seaweed! Seashell!

DORA. Ha! Hermit crab!

TY. Hermit crab!

DORA. I think I see you!

TY. Barely!

DORA. You're here.

TY. Yeah — a hideous mistake but — here I am. *(They are a few feet away from each other, though both looking somewhat past each other, as though still indistinct.)*

DORA. God it's so dark.

TY. No moon. No stars.

DORA. There's clouds.

TY. Are there clouds?

DORA. You can tell 'cuz the sky feels so low. Can you feel how low the sky is? Look up.

TY. *(Looking up.)* It is low.

DORA. You can feel it, right?

TY. It's colder than I thought.

DORA. It gets warmer.

TY. Ha, does it?

DORA. You're really cold?

TY. Shivering.

DORA. Come closer. *(She moves somewhat blindly towards him, while he remains relatively still, groping a bit dumbly.)* Am I — I'm right/in

TY. Yeah, I'm right/here

DORA. Hold my hand to stay warm.

TY. Hold your — where — but I can't/see

DORA. Find my hand, in the/water

TY. I can't/even

DORA. Just move your hand around … *(Beneath the water, both hands search. And connect.)* There!

TY. Yeah!

DORA. Found it. *(Silence. The two look at each other, still significantly obscured by darkness so that though they are inches away from each other, they stare intensely as if far apart from the other. Their hands stay clutched.)* Your face …

TY. My face?

DORA. I can't see you …

TY. I'm here …

DORA. You are … God.

TY. What?

DORA. Just feel it.

TY. What? *(Dora wraps her arm around Ty's waist, and moves behind him, clutching him. She sways with the gentle tide.)*

DORA. There. *(Dora presses against Ty, swaying; he begins to sway as well.)* Do you feel it? *(Now they are swaying in unison to the tide.)*

TY. I think …

DORA. Close your eyes … *(A beat. He does. The swaying grows more close, more intense, though it continues to be gentle.)* Do you feel it? …

TY. Mmm …

DORA. Right? … *(Ty opens his eyes. He turns his head to look at Dora, whose eyes are closed. He stares at her a long while.)*

DORA. Can I tell you something, Ty? *(Ty turns back, closes his eyes.)*

TY. — Sure.

DORA. It's a secret …

TY. A — secret?

DORA. You don't have to say anything.

TY. Wh — what?

DORA. A secret from that night at the bar …

TY. What?

DORA. Shhh. *(Dora, eyes still closed, still clutching Ty, begins to kiss his neck. Again he opens his eyes and looks, as if about to speak. She continues to kiss him with great feeling. Then he closes his eyes and arches towards her. Their lips meet. Abruptly, he pulls away. Dora opens her eyes and looks at him. He stares back, somewhat inscrutable, as if about to speak but hesitant. Slowly their gaze entwines, and Ty turns away. She approaches him. She puts her hand on Ty's chest. He turns to her and with a sense of inevitability and deep communion they embrace. They kiss. Then Ty pulls back, ever so slightly, and whispers:)*

TY. I can't.

DORA. Shhh.

TY. Dora. *(She continues to kiss his neck.)* I know, Dora.

DORA. Mmm … *(She runs her hand up and down his chest, towards his groin.)*

TY. Oh God — *(She puts her hand beneath his boxer shorts.)* Dora —

DORA. Mmmm … *(She continues to kiss his neck.)*

TY. I know — Dora — No — oh God — *oh* — *(Ty releases from Dora almost violently. Her eyes open. Ty strides back to shore, through the thick water. Dora watches him till he is off. On shore, Ty dresses. In the ocean, Dora stares blankly ahead. Then suddenly she plunges herself under the surface of the water, and hangs there, lifeless, peaceful. Just as suddenly she emerges, almost violently, from beneath the ocean. She sucks in air and chokes, then takes in a monstrous, gasping breath. Slowly her breathing normalizes, and she starts her way out of the vast dark ocean to shore. On shore, Ty sits, dressed, his head in his knees. Dora comes onto the beach and moves to her clothes. Silently, she starts to dress. Ty picks up his head and watches her. She turns and sees. Conversationally:)*

DORA. I do *not* wanna work tomorrow.

TY. What time are you working?

DORA. Morning. The corporate people are sending all these people down — it's this thing they do after a robbery, this whole fucking interview thing. But since they didn't get any money it shouldn't be that bad, hopefully.

TY. Right.

DORA. You should come in sometime. I got this stack of free rental coupons for dissatisfied customers, but we can use them for whatever.

TY. Cool.

DORA. Someone was telling me ... *(She's fully dressed.)* You can rent movies online now or something? Do you do that? *(Dora looks to Ty. His head is bowed again.)* Ty? *(Ty looks up to her. A beat.)* What's wrong?

TY. I know it was Edward that — did this to your face, Dora. *(Pause. Dora chuckles.)*

DORA. What are you talking about?

TY. He came to me the night — he shot/himself.

DORA. You know — I gotta work tomorrow for like/twelve hours

TY. He told me he needed ten thousand dollars — he wouldn't say for what,/but he seemed really desperate — and

DORA. He always needed money —

TY. He told me he was going to rob you. *(Pause.)* He was really high, he was fucked up, I knew I should have done something but I just — wrote him a check and — I ... they didn't find it on him so. I guess — after he went to the Blockbuster he — that's when he decided to — that's when he came to the beach and killed himself. *(Suddenly Dora clutches her jaw.)*

DORA. Nnnnh. Nnnnnh. Nnnnnh. *(Ty rises. Dora breathes. Then another wave of pain.)* Ahhhh. Ahhhhhhh. *(Ty moves towards Dora.)*

TY. Let me take you home — *(Ty reaches out to her. Dora slaps his arm away, her purse flung off her arm. Ty takes a shocked step back.)* What's wrong? *(Dora doesn't answer. She slowly removes her hand from her jaw. She gains her balance, then starts to move to where her purse is.*

Ty takes a few steps as if to retrieve it for her, but she shakes her head "no." She reaches her purse and in agony, sits down. She takes out a pill. She manages to open her mouth ever so slightly; she bends her head back and drops the pill onto her tongue. She tries to swallow; gags badly; then forces it down. Ty takes a step towards her. She looks at him. They stare at each other for a moment. Then she turns away from him and looks out at the ocean. Ty watches her for a moment, and then turns and leaves the beach, off. Dora does not turn to see that he is gone.)

SCENE FOUR

Day. Dora approaches Ty, who is sitting on the beach. He is wearing headphones. So is she. She sees Ty and takes off her headphones.

DORA. Ty. *(He doesn't respond. She sees he's wearing headphones. She moves in front of him and smiles. He looks up. Eventually he sees her, and takes his headphones off.)* Hey!
TY. Hi!
DORA. Sorry I'm late. I would have called but I don't have your cell. *(He rises.)*
TY. It's okay.
DORA. What are you listening to?
TY. Oh — just — a mix I burned — different stuff.
DORA. Trade for a second?
TY. — Sure!
DORA. You're gonna hate this. Okay. *(They sit down and switch headphones. Both sit and listen to each other's discs. Dora rocks out a little. Ty laughs, grooves to Dora's music.)* IT'S GOOD. WHAT IS IT.
TY. IT'S THIS FRIEND OF MINE. CREATES IT ALL HIM-SELF, JUST HIM, A KEYBOARD AND A MAC.
DORA. COOL. — DO YOU HATE MINE.
TY. WHAT'S THERE TO HATE ABOUT CYNDI LAUPER.
(Dora laughs. They listen a few more seconds. Then Dora takes the

headphones off, and Ty follows. They hand them back to each other.)
DORA. Your friend is good. Is he from here?
TY. Yeah, he's in school here. Doesn't go to class much, spends all day writing songs on his computer. Big into ecstasy, kind of a drug freak.
DORA. Tell me about it. It took me so long to get off that Vicodin.
TY. Yeah?
DORA. Do you know you can get it on the Internet? My last refill ran out and I was freaking, and then this guy was like, I get Vicodin online. They have like online pharmacies and Doctors talk to you on the phone and stuff, and just prescribe it. So then *he* got me some ...
TY. But you're — you're off them?
DORA. Yeah. I'm basically fine. I still have a little back thing, but I do this water therapy, 'cuz the water helps it supposedly.
TY. Are you in a rehabilitation program or? ...
DORA. No, they just showed me how, I do it on my own.
TY. In the ocean?
DORA. It's too cold now. I've been using the pool at the casino, actually.
TY. Oh.
DORA. I went to this acupuncturist too for a while, for my back.
TY. Oh yeah?
DORA. It really helped. They rake it in, those guys. Good line of business to be in. Everyone's back is a wreck, right? Nobody can walk in this country.
TY. Or sleep.
DORA. Ambien for that. You like Ambien?
TY. Never had it.
DORA. Ambien/Vicodin combo ... like peanut butter and jelly.
(Ty laughs. Short pause.)
TY. You look — amazing.
DORA. I do?
TY. Like — nothing happened.
DORA. They did a good job, right? When they did the operation on my nose, they actually, I think they made it better than before. The girls at work are all like, Did you get a nose job?
TY. Wow.

DORA. I swear to God. I thought the rest of my life, people were gonna look at me, like, "What the fuck happened to her?" Like one of those people.

TY. Right.

DORA. 'Cuz I see those women. They come in to Blockbuster. Alone. The ugliest guy can come in, there's some woman with him. Ugly women, forget it. I got two new teeth too, sec? Discolored, just like my real ones. *(She bares her teeth.)*

TY. Watch out, she can bite. *(Short pause.)*

DORA. What about you?

TY. What about me.

DORA. What's going on, player!

TY. *(Laughs.)* Not much. *(Short pause.)* I've — missed you. *(Short pause.)* Been thinking of quitting my job.

DORA. You're kidding.

TY. Thinking about it.

DORA. Why?

TY. I'm just tired of it. There must be something else I can do.

DORA. Don't quit your job.

TY. No?

DORA. No. You have a good job, Ty. *(Short pause.)*

TY. Just something I'm thinking about. *(Pause.)*

DORA. I'm going to this therapist.

TY. Really?

DORA. Yeah. It's good, you know? We talk a lot about — we talk about everything that happened and. *(Short pause.)*

TY. It's okay. *(Dora smiles at Ty and looks away. Then Dora's cell phone rings. She checks it, then shuts it off. Pause.)*

DORA. I'm sorry about that night Ty. And not calling you and. I'm sorry. *(Dora's cell phone rings again. She answers.)* Hey. Yeah. I'm running late. At the store, we're rearranging the whole store and it's taking forever. No. Soon. Okay. *(Hanging up.)* Sorry. Meeting someone later ...

TY. It's okay.

DORA. The last thing I expected.

TY. — What?

DORA. Remember that guy I told you about? Martin? Who works at the casino, Eddie's friend?

TY. Yeah?

DORA. I guess he was all upset, like, that I wasn't at Eddie's wake, and so he called a couple days after to check on me. Turns out he's like this really cool guy … *(Pause. Ty looks away.)* My therapist thinks it's a really good thing for/me

TY. I'm sure it is. *(Pause.)*

DORA. I'm not — I'm not gonna say some stupid thing to you that isn't true. *(Pause.)* I don't/want to

TY. I actually — have to get somewhere, so.

DORA. Oh. *(Ty rises.)* Can I get your cell?

TY. Calling me at home is the best way/to

DORA. Well — give it to me anyway.

TY. Why? *(Pause.)*

DORA. — I don't wanna say anything stupid to you, Ty.

TY. So don't. *(Pause.)*

DORA. — I want what I have to say to you to come out right.

TY. Fine. Call me when you figure it out. *(Ty starts to go. Dora rises.)*

DORA. You know that's not how I — wait, Ty. *(He stops and turns.)* Forget all that, okay? There's one/thing.

TY. *Forget* it?

DORA. Just — there's something I need you to tell me. *(Pause.)* I need you to tell me the truth. 'Cuz I know you know it.

TY. What? *(Pause.)*

DORA. When I think about that night. I think about how you said you should have done something. How you should have done something but you just let him go. *(Pause.)* Sometimes I think about things *I* did to him. Things *I* said. And my therapist, she says, she always says, "It's not your fault that he killed himself. It's not your fault, Dora." But. Like. What *I* think is, Whose fault is it then? *(Pause.)* Because. In a way. It *is* my fault. *(Pause.)* Is it? *(Dora and Ty look at each other. Pause. Dora turns away from Ty, and looks out at the ocean. Ty turns away, towards the shore. Then Ty turns to Dora. He is quietly crying. He watches her looking out at the ocean. Then, as if sensing his eyes on her, she turns to him. A long silence. Then:)*

TY. (No.) *(Pause.)*

DORA. (Thank you.) *(Hold.)*

End of Play

PROPERTY LIST

Ten dollars (ED)
Purse, pills (DORA)
Headphones, portable CD players (DORA, TY)
Cell phone (DORA)

NEW PLAYS

★ **MONTHS ON END by Craig Pospisil.** In comic scenes, one for each month of the year, we follow the intertwined worlds of a circle of friends and family whose lives are poised between happiness and heartbreak. "…a triumph…these twelve vignettes all form crucial pieces in the eternal puzzle known as human relationships, an area in which the playwright displays an assured knowledge that spans deep sorrow to unbounded happiness." *–Ann Arbor News.* "…rings with emotional truth, humor…[an] endearing contemplation on love…entertaining and satisfying." *–Oakland Press.* [5M, 5W] ISBN: 0-8222-1892-5

★ **GOOD THING by Jessica Goldberg.** Brings us into the households of John and Nancy Roy, forty-something high-school guidance counselors whose marriage has been increasingly on the rocks and Dean and Mary, recent graduates struggling to make their way in life. "…a blend of gritty social drama, poetic humor and unsubtle existential contemplation…" *–Variety.* [3M, 3W] ISBN: 0-8222-1869-0

★ **THE DEAD EYE BOY by Angus MacLachlan.** Having fallen in love at their Narcotics Anonymous meeting, Billy and Shirley-Diane are striving to overcome the past together. But their relationship is complicated by the presence of Sorin, Shirley-Diane's fourteen-year-old son, a damaged reminder of her dark past. "…a grim, insightful portrait of an unmoored family…" *–NY Times.* "MacLachlan's play isn't for the squeamish, but then, tragic stories delivered at such an unrelenting fever pitch rarely are." *–Variety.* [1M, 1W, 1 boy] ISBN: 0-8222-1844-5

★ **[SIC] by Melissa James Gibson.** In adjacent apartments three young, ambitious neighbors come together to discuss, flirt, argue, share their dreams and plan their futures with unequal degrees of deep hopefulness and abject despair. "A work…concerned with the sound and power of language…" *–NY Times.* "…a wonderfully original take on urban friendship and the comedy of manners—a *Design for Living* for our times…" *–NY Observer.* [3M, 2W] ISBN: 0-8222-1872-0

★ **LOOKING FOR NORMAL by Jane Anderson.** Roy and Irma's twenty-five-year marriage is thrown into turmoil when Roy confesses that he is actually a woman trapped in a man's body, forcing the couple to wrestle with the meaning of their marriage and the delicate dynamics of family. "Jane Anderson's bittersweet transgender domestic comedy-drama …is thoughtful and touching and full of wit and wisdom. A real audience pleaser." *–Hollywood Reporter.* [5M, 4W] ISBN: 0-8222-1857-7

★ **ENDPAPERS by Thomas McCormack.** The regal Joshua Maynard, the old and ailing head of a mid-sized, family-owned book-publishing house in New York City, must name a successor. One faction in the house backs a smart, "pragmatic" manager, the other faction a smart, "sensitive" editor and both factions fear what the other's man could do to this house— and to them. "If Kaufman and Hart had undertaken a comedy about the publishing business, they might have written *Endpapers*…a breathlessly fast, funny, and thoughtful comedy …keeps you amused, guessing, and often surprised…profound in its empathy for the paradoxes of human nature." *–NY Magazine.* [7M, 4W] ISBN: 0-8222-1908-5

★ **THE PAVILION by Craig Wright.** By turns poetic and comic, romantic and philosophical, this play asks old lovers to face the consequences of difficult choices made long ago. "The script's greatest strength lies in the genuineness of its feeling." *–Houston Chronicle.* "Wright's perceptive, gently witty writing makes this familiar situation fresh and thoroughly involving." *–Philadelphia Inquirer.* [2M, 1W (flexible casting)] ISBN: 0-8222-1898-4

DRAMATISTS PLAY SERVICE, INC.
440 Park Avenue South, New York, NY 10016 212-683-8960 Fax 212-213-1539
postmaster@dramatists.com   www.dramatists.com

NEW PLAYS

★ **BE AGGRESSIVE by Annie Weisman.** Vista Del Sol is paradise, sandy beaches, avocado-lined streets. But for seventeen-year-old cheerleader Laura, everything changes when her mother is killed in a car crash, and she embarks on a journey to the Spirit Institute of the South where she can learn "cheer" with Bible belt intensity. "...filled with lingual gymnastics...stylized rapid-fire dialogue..." –*Variety.* "...a new, exciting, and unique voice in the American theatre..." –*BackStage West.* [1M, 4W, extras] ISBN: 0-8222-1894-1

★ **FOUR by Christopher Shinn.** Four people struggle desperately to connect in this quiet, sophisticated, moving drama. "...smart, broken-hearted...Mr. Shinn has a precocious and forgiving sense of how power shifts in the game of sexual pursuit...He promises to be a playwright to reckon with..." –*NY Times.* "A voice emerges from an American place. It's got humor, sadness and a fresh and touching rhythm that tell of the loneliness and secrets of life...[a] poetic, haunting play." –*NY Post.* [3M, 1W] ISBN: 0-8222-1850-X

★ **WONDER OF THE WORLD by David Lindsay-Abaire.** A madcap picaresque involving Niagara Falls, a lonely tour-boat captain, a pair of bickering private detectives and a husband's dirty little secret. "Exceedingly whimsical and playfully wicked. Winning and genial. A top-drawer production." –*NY Times.* "Full frontal lunacy is on display. A most assuredly fresh and hilarious tragicomedy of marital discord run amok...absolutely hysterical..." –*Variety.* [3M, 4W (doubling)] ISBN: 0-8222-1863-1

★ **QED by Peter Parnell.** Nobel Prize-winning physicist and all-around genius Richard Feynman holds forth with captivating wit and wisdom in this fascinating biographical play that originally starred Alan Alda. "QED is a seductive mix of science, human affections, moral courage, and comic eccentricity. It reflects on, among other things, death, the absence of God, travel to an unexplored country, the pleasures of drumming, and the need to know and understand." –*NY Magazine.* "Its rhythms correspond to the way that people—even geniuses—approach and avoid highly emotional issues, and it portrays Feynman with affection and awe." –*The New Yorker.* [1M, 1W] ISBN: 0-8222-1924-7

★ **UNWRAP YOUR CANDY by Doug Wright.** Alternately chilling and hilarious, this deliciously macabre collection of four bedtime tales for adults is guaranteed to keep you awake for nights on end. "Engaging and intellectually satisfying...a treat to watch." –*NY Times.* "Fiendishly clever. Mordantly funny and chilling. Doug Wright teases, freezes and zaps us." –*Village Voice.* "Four bite-size plays that bite back." –*Variety.* [flexible casting] ISBN: 0-8222-1871-2

★ **FURTHER THAN THE FURTHEST THING by Zinnie Harris.** On a remote island in the middle of the Atlantic secrets are buried. When the outside world comes calling, the islanders find their world blown apart from the inside as well as beyond. "Harris winningly produces an intimate and poetic, as well as political, family saga." –*Independent (London).* "Harris' enthralling adventure of a play marks a departure from stale, well-furrowed theatrical terrain." –*Evening Standard (London).* [3M, 2W] ISBN: 0-8222-1874-7

★ **THE DESIGNATED MOURNER by Wallace Shawn.** The story of three people living in a country where what sort of books people like to read and how they choose to amuse themselves becomes both firmly personal and unexpectedly entangled with questions of survival. "This is a playwright who does not just tell you what it is like to be arrested at night by goons or to fall morally apart and become an aimless yet weirdly contented ghost yourself. He has the originality to make you feel it." –*Times (London).* "A fascinating play with beautiful passages of writing..." –*Variety.* [2M, 1W] ISBN: 0-8222-1848-8

DRAMATISTS PLAY SERVICE, INC.
440 Park Avenue South, New York, NY 10016 212-683-8960 Fax 212-213-1539
postmaster@dramatists.com www.dramatists.com

NEW PLAYS

★ **SHEL'S SHORTS by Shel Silverstein.** Lauded poet, songwriter and author of children's books, the incomparable Shel Silverstein's short plays are deeply infused with the same wicked sense of humor that made him famous. "...[a] childlike honesty and twisted sense of humor." *—Boston Herald.* "...terse dialogue and an absurdity laced with a tang of dread give [*Shel's Shorts*] more than a trace of Samuel Beckett's comic existentialism." *—Boston Phoenix.* [flexible casting] ISBN: 0-8222-1897-6

★ **AN ADULT EVENING OF SHEL SILVERSTEIN by Shel Silverstein.** Welcome to the darkly comic world of Shel Silverstein, a world where nothing is as it seems and where the most innocent conversation can turn menacing in an instant. These ten imaginative plays vary widely in content, but the style is unmistakable. "...[*An Adult Evening*] shows off Silverstein's virtuosic gift for wordplay...[and] sends the audience out...with a clear appreciation of human nature as perverse and laughable." *—NY Times.* [flexible casting] ISBN: 0-8222-1873-9

★ **WHERE'S MY MONEY? by John Patrick Shanley.** A caustic and sardonic vivisection of the institution of marriage, laced with the author's inimitable razor-sharp wit. "...Shanley's gift for acid-laced one-liners and emotionally tumescent exchanges is certainly potent..." *—Variety.* "...lively, smart, occasionally scary and rich in reverse wisdom." *—NY Times.* [3M, 3W] ISBN: 0-8222-1865-8

★ **A FEW STOUT INDIVIDUALS by John Guare.** A wonderfully screwy comedy-drama that figures Ulysses S. Grant in the throes of writing his memoirs, surrounded by a cast of fantastical characters, including the Emperor and Empress of Japan, the opera star Adelina Patti and Mark Twain. "Guare's smarts, passion and creativity skyrocket to awesome heights..." *—Star Ledger.* "...precisely the kind of good new play that you might call an everyday miracle...every minute of it is fresh and newly alive..." *—Village Voice.* [10M, 3W] ISBN: 0-8222-1907-7

★ **BREATH, BOOM by Kia Corthron.** A look at fourteen years in the life of Prix, a Bronx native, from her ruthless girl-gang leadership at sixteen through her coming to maturity at thirty. "...vivid world, believable and eye-opening, a place worthy of a dramatic visit, where no one would want to live but many have to." *—NY Times.* "...rich with humor, terse vernacular strength and gritty detail..." *—Variety.* [1M, 9W] ISBN: 0-8222-1849-6

★ **THE LATE HENRY MOSS by Sam Shepard.** Two antagonistic brothers, Ray and Earl, are brought together after their father, Henry Moss, is found dead in his seedy New Mexico home in this classic Shepard tale. "...His singular gift has been for building mysteries out of the ordinary ingredients of American family life..." *—NY Times.* "...rich moments ...Shepard finds gold." *—LA Times.* [7M, 1W] ISBN: 0-8222-1858-5

★ **THE CARPETBAGGER'S CHILDREN by Horton Foote.** One family's history spanning from the Civil War to WWII is recounted by three sisters in evocative, intertwining monologues. "...bittersweet music—[a] rhapsody of ambivalence...in its modest, garrulous way...theatrically daring." *—The New Yorker.* [3W] ISBN: 0-8222-1843-7

★ **THE NINA VARIATIONS by Steven Dietz.** In this funny, fierce and heartbreaking homage to *The Seagull*, Dietz puts Chekhov's star-crossed lovers in a room and doesn't let them out. "A perfect little jewel of a play..." *—Shepherdstown Chronicle.* "...a delightful revelation of a writer at play; and also an odd, haunting, moving theater piece of lingering beauty." *—Eastside Journal (Seattle).* [1M, 1W (flexible casting)] ISBN: 0-8222-1891-7

DRAMATISTS PLAY SERVICE, INC.
440 Park Avenue South, New York, NY 10016 212-683-8960 Fax 212-213-1539
postmaster@dramatists.com www.dramatists.com